Altered
at the
Altar

Shade Salako

Altered at the Altar

Dedication

This book is dedicated to my dear Heavenly Father, the Almighty God whose breath is in me, without whom my life would have been incomplete.

Jesus Christ my strength in weakness, my hope in despair, my Saviour and Redeemer.

Precious Holy Spirit, my lifelong teacher, my helper and best friend.

The glory and the lifter of my head. By Your help I will keep growing stronger every day until I have handed the baton over to the coming generation.

Acknowledgement

With much gratitude to the Almighty God, I celebrate all the people that have made commendable impacts in my life during the past five decades of my life. Sincere gratitude to God for my beginning in the hands of my beloved parents. Mr and Mrs Gabriel Olaleye, and to all siblings. I'm so blessed growing up together with you, it was such great fun!

To my husband, Adewale, my crown. I'm glad my heart said yes when you called. You taught me what is true and sacrificial love in marriage. Thank you for your untiring support in always ensuring to make things right, your dauntless courage through the experiences we both shared together, my captain, I love you dearly.

To my "three wise men" Joshua, Joseph and Jonathan, it is a great privilege for me; I have enjoyed and will continue to enjoy every moment of serving you all.

And to Joan my blessed daughter, your evergreen memory will always be in my heart.

Special thanks to all the impact of the Word upon my life through all God's faithful shepherds who have taught, mentored and guided me. I have been strengthened by the foundational teachings, guidance and discipline of a long list of great Apostles of God that I have encountered in my life during the past few decades, too numerous to mention. May He who has called you greatly reward your labour of love.

To all my brothers and sisters of the militant church worldwide. May the Lord Jesus find us worthy when He appears in the clouds.

Maranatha!

Foreword

In this present age, many people are still searching for the fundamentals of life such as peace, identity, and purpose but the challenge is that many are looking for it either in the wrong places or with the wrong means or methods, but all these and many more are embedded in the message of salvation.

Everyone's journey from darkness to light or out of a horrible pit of the miry clay to setting one's feet upon a rock, and establishing one's goings should not be cumbersome or complicated as it is often presented or presumed, the message of salvation is a simple one.

This book "Altered at the Altar " simplifies the process, precepts by precepts with the author's life experiences, written in simple words for everyone to understand and follow.

It is recommended for anyone that is thirsty and longing to be 'Altered on the Altar' by the Almighty God, the Creator of all creations.

Pastor Tosin Popoola

Preface

A feeling of inadequacy enveloped me when the Lord first laid the thought of writing the contents of this book in my heart. I felt I needed some sort of validation to write these things I knew nothing about; at least that was my thought until the Lord nudged me. He unfolded His plans, and His desire to see all men liberated from the grips of ignorance because it is a known fact, confirmed by scriptures that a man's ignorance is his own destruction.

"For my people are destroyed for lack of knowledge..." Hosea 4:6a KJV

To lack knowledge is like being in a dark place, and this results in ignorance in all ramifications. Jesus brings light to our lives and in his life is all freedom.

"Then you will know the truth, and the truth will set you free..." John 8:32 NIV

I allowed God's intent to supersede my feelings and needs and discovered afterwards that although every single human being desires validation one way or the other, our utmost joy is derived when we fulfil His purpose.

And so, with this understanding came an end to the hesitation that stalled me on my tracks because to me, the assignment of writing this message is one that is completely divine!

Having knowledge and a vivid understanding of our coexistence in this world should be the goal of every one of us because it acts as a guide to the manner in which we behave in all dimensions of relationship and companionship.

This book will open your eyes to the essence of relationships through all walks of life and highlight the natural man as a spirit, soul and body.

The nature of man as a tripartite being is relatively suggestive that likes are alike and relationships would be expressed in three parts. Man is a spirit being, he has a soul; an enclosure of the mind and intellectual capacity and all these are encased in a body.

God, on the other hand, is a Spirit whose expression exists severally. The gift of His spirit in us unfolds the bliss of an amazing connection, that although it is evident that man could be joined in flesh and soul in relationship with others in the natural realm, he can only best relate with God in a spiritual ambience. Therefore, it is the spirit of man that is drawn to relate with God first of all at the point of salvation.

"But the person who is joined to the Lord is one spirit with Him". 1 Cor. 6:17. (NLT)

"No one can know a person's thoughts except that person's own spirit, and no one can know God's thoughts except God's own Spirit. And we have received God's Spirit (not the world's spirit), so we can know the wonderful things God has freely given us." 1 Cor. 2:11-12 (NLT)

It is this wonderful gift of salvation that calls man to encounter abundant life as it ushers one into an infinite alluring relationship with God, contrary to the belief that it is only a call to a life of misery and depravity.

Everyone needs to understand the essence of having a genuine relationship with God. I invite you to accept Jesus as your Lord and Saviour. You are simply required to acknowledge your sins before Him, ask and receive forgiveness and accept the gift of eternal life.

Shade Salako

Contents

"

An Altar,
A place where destiny takes a recourse, where supernatural
and the natural meet, a place where supernatural
transactions take place

"

Introduction

There are countless lives in the world today that at some point down the journeys of their lives have either voluntarily taken a wrong turn, or been forced down the wrong track. A wrong decision, a wrong choice has set them on a collision course with destruction. If you are such a person, I bring you good news today that the Almighty God is set to alter your life at His altar.

To **alter** simply means to change, reform, orientate and to transform into another figure. In this context, to recourse. This is very important because the corrupted nature which we inherited from Adam has set humanity on a collision course with destruction and it needs to be changed in order to restore the relationship.

An altar is a sacred place for sacrifices and gifts offered up to God. Right from the beginning of time, God had always impressed in the hearts of people to offer Him sacrifices on altars. It does not only refer to that designated place in a temple building, or shrines, or churches where religious ceremonies are performed, but there is more to it. It is a sacred place, a location, an instance or occasion where divinity meets with humanity.

It is a call to the personality trait of Jesus on earth as both God and man. It is a place of settlement and agreement, and of exchange, a place of encounter.

God's altar is a place of power, a point of contact for sacred fellowship and communion with the Divine God, it could be anywhere from your secret bedroom, on the bus, in the airport, cafe, office, prison or the most unusual of places, so long as your heart is connected.

For instance, the thief that met Christ on the cross at the point of death, while his mate hurled insults at the Saviour, he was right to acknowledge and ask for mercy. He understood that while it was too late for him to go to the physical altar at the temple, right there Christ before him represented the altar where his destiny was open to being changed. And *Carpe diem!* He seized the moment, a divine opportunity; every wrong he had written against him all along just got cleaned out in exchange for eternity with Christ Jesus. What a bliss!

"One of the criminals hanging beside him scoffed, "So you're the Messiah, are you? Prove it by saving yourself—and us, too, while you're at it!" But the other criminal protested, "Don't you fear God even when you have been sentenced to die? . We deserve to die for our crimes, but this man hasn't done anything wrong." Then he said, "Jesus, remember me when you come into your Kingdom." And Jesus replied, "I assure you, today you will be with me in paradise." Luke 23:39-43(NIV)

The story is recorded of a religious woman who encountered Christ at the well in John 4:7-26. The well in this instance would be an altar – a place of encounter.

"Sir," the woman said, "you have nothing to draw with and the well is deep. Where can you get this living water? Are you greater than our father Jacob, who gave us the well and drank from it himself, as did also his sons and his livestock?" Jesus answered, "Everyone who drinks this water will be thirsty again, but whoever drinks the water I give them will never thirst. Indeed, the water I give them will become in them a spring of water welling up to eternal life." The woman said to him, "Sir, give me this water so that I won't get thirsty and have to keep coming here to draw water." John 4:11 -15 NIV

When she realised who He was, she surrendered to Him totally (her life was altered in such a way that even the people in her community were changed). This is the kind of life we should emulate, there is more in Christ than all the riches of the world. Invariably we encounter God every day, it then depends on our disposition of who God is. The woman's encounter with Jesus altered her shameful past to a joyous testimony. Her hideous history was revealed, shamed and altered to an expression of glory. "Come and see!" she gladly summoned all to come and meet with her Saviour. The Altar is a place to remain at the feet of the Master where brokenness is a constant, restoration and realignment is lifelong until Christ returns. We are in a perpetual process of being perfected into the fullness of His being. The longer you stay in his presence the more you experience transformation, you become more and more like Him because He is there, working at the wheel. Each time you appear before Him you realise that you want more and more. You yearn for a touch that will usher you into a greater realm. It must be an everyday appearance and not a once occasion visit.

Then he said to the crowd: "Whoever wants to be my disciple must deny themselves and take up their cross daily and follow me. Luke 9:23 (NIV)

Paul also admonished the people in Rome to present themselves to God.

"Therefore, I urge you, brothers and sisters, in view of God's mercy, to offer your bodies as a living sacrifice, holy and pleasing to God—this is your true and proper worship. Do not conform to the pattern of this world, but be transformed by the renewing of your mind. Then you will be able to test and approve what God's will is—his good, pleasing and perfect will" Romans 12:1-2 NIV

You may have been a church goer long enough, but if there seems to be a vacuum that only God can fill. It is time to come before your Creator, to hold unto Him and where possible wrestle like Jacob until your desired change comes.

The Bible gave examples of men like Abraham, Moses, Apostle Paul who experienced change varyingly as they encountered the Almighty at different stages and instances of their lives. In this age and time, God still remains the same, calling us to Himself. God gives us the liberty of using our will to determine the future He desires for us and to embrace the plans He has for us.

The concept of raising altars to God however has been adulterated by the devil; and we have seen over the years evil altars being erected to sacrifice to idols and false gods. This practice has been handed over from generation to generation down to our ancestors who would have raised certain strange altars for us. These altars, if they still exist, would have been speaking to one's destiny and responsible for how that life is directed.

The purpose of this book therefore is to announce that the time to consciously make a decision for yourself allowing God to alter the altar of darkness and bring light to prevail over darkness in our lives is now!

1Peter 2:9 says:

"But you are not like that, for you are a chosen people. You are royal priests, a holy nation, God's very own possession. As a result, you can show others the goodness of God, for he called you out of darkness into his wonderful light."

God is a Changer therefore, know where you are at, so as to be able to trust God with your life in humble surrender. This is the starting point to total freedom, being overtaken by His mind. We love changes from day to day so much more than the weather, we need to trust in the one Unchanging Changer to make it happen.

And so, He invites us to His altar; a place to reason and settle our destinies.

Isaiah 1:18 (KJV) says: *"Come let us reason together, though your sins be as scarlet, they shall be as white as snow."*

First of all, come! An invitation to the place of encounter, you are the best gift desired because to be so precious, every other thing you chose to bring along with you comes second.

Take a moment to reason along with the King now before you proceed into the next pages of this book, answer this call, it is an invitation and enjoy an unending bliss. Pray if you will:

Dear God, I believe in the life, death and resurrection of your only begotten Son Jesus. I accept this call today as I invite You to please come into my heart, I forsake my old ways, please forgive all my sins and cleanse me from the inside out through Jesus Christ. Help me to live according to Your ways from now on. Amen.

Now that you have said this prayer, you are set for a lifelong relationship with the Almighty God and ready to embrace the revelation in the pages of this book!

"

*The whole existence of man is
for relationships, requiring a
level of connection with one
another*

"

Chapter 1: Relationship Matters

The Oxford Languages dictionary defines relationship as the way in which two or more people or things are connected, or simply put, the state of being connected.

However, the way relationships are viewed across the globe differs and so are the values placed on them. The whole existence of man is for relationships, requiring a level of connection with one another. There are relationships in every sphere of life including inanimate objects; iron and stone, the earth and herbs, the ocean and fish, nations to nations, etc.

Relationships exist to meet a need or fill a vacuum, such as a husband and wife in a marriage, or a mentor and his protégé in coaching, and many other relationships in life. It is important to note that we are all trapped in this world wide web of interdependence by God's design. Therefore, the most prudent and logical decision for mankind is to first embrace God's tremendous love offered by Christ because this would by far be the best deal anyone can broker for themselves. It was for this reason Jesus Christ; our Lord and Saviour died to redeem and reconcile the fallen man from a strained relationship with God.

We learnt from the Bible that Adam, the first man disobeyed God and by this he lost the bond of human kinship with God. But Jesus Christ; the second Adam, became the ransom for the redemption of man. God's love flows from Him to all men so that it becomes obvious to see a relationship with God forming the climax of every other good relationship, I mean real good ones.

"For as by one man's disobedience many were made sinners, so by the one obedience of one man many shall be made righteous." Romans 5 :19 KJV

"This first man Adam and the last man Jesus Christ."

Every relationship begins at some point; some with boundaries, others without any boundary at all. But the relationship between God the Creator and the whole creation is boundless and has long existed before time. And although this knowledge may not be known by many at first instance, with time and careful observation, we come to the realisation that nothing really makes sense until we get reconnected back to the real source.

Ecclesiastes 3:11 tells us that God planted eternity in the human heart.

There is a time and place in life for us to be joined back to the Lord, the trigger is mostly when we begin to feel a vacuum which nothing else but God can fill. When life takes a toll on a man irrespective of fame, wealth, substance or power, there is such emptiness that brings to bear a dying need for a saviour. Such a place, I would liken it to an Altar.

An Altar,

A point where humanity meets with divinity

An Altar,

A place where destiny takes a recourse

An Altar,

Music plays the tunes, to transforming beats for change;

change of direction

And whosoever desires, dances to the music divine

It portrays true connection

Embraces truthfulness

Exudes compassion

And reveals the reality

That relationships matter, life becomes meaningful.

The way in which we perceive this truth is very important and appreciably more relieving when we open our hearts in order to grasp the genuine cue from the fountain of life.

When it comes to the subject of relationships, no one element stands in isolation but all are linked one to another. Just look around you, consider the relationship between the seed sown in the ground, the sun that brings heat, the rain that waters it, the dung and the worms helping to cultivate, the produce and the farmer and the list is endless. All these reflect the benefits of relationships in all aspects of life, these are the blessings of God Almighty.

Relationships can grow into a strong bond if well nurtured. While some who don't really understand the essence of this, tend to walk away as things ruffle up, others endure the heat and make an effort to ensure that the benefits are enjoyed by all. A good relationship will thrive on account of the pursuit of knowledge, purpose and commitment from all parties. Even so, the boundary lines of some relationships are better defined because they only exist for a purpose and for space of time after which it gradually fades away.

However, we need to have a sound relationship with God if we must stand in dominion and against the continual darts of the adversary. Without God, we are in the real sense, lifeless, hopeless and helpless.

Surprisingly I have heard countless times, some ungracious remarks from people who disregard God's selfless act of love and sacrifice, in that Christ died for the sins of the whole world. This suggests a vague knowledge of who God is and His reckless love for mankind, such ignorance or rather unacceptance sterns from some painful episodes experienced by some and blamed solely on God. I have heard remarks such as "I don't need the love of God".

Isn't it amazing that God did not seek anyone's opinion before He chose to love us? He did it freely to save us from the impending danger of hell and destruction.

The truth is that we all need God and cannot deny this just because of some embittered experiences of life. Yes! I do quite understand that there may have been times of distress, disappointments and discouragements in life but trust that God had always been closer than could have been imagined, He is always there to catch us from falling, to soothe our wounds, to heal and to restore and heal our brokenness. So, whenever a situation arises that brings pain, or triggers bad emotions, always remember that there is never any distance away from HIM.

I have felt hurt, been distressed, disappointed, guilty and alone sometimes; and although it seemed like a dark place to be, I realised that I was not alone then and have never been because God walked me through each step of the way.

My reassuring words to everyone reading this book is that if you have been through any kind of trouble, your scars are a beautiful reminder of the blessedness of being alive today and telling your story will definitely inspire others. This should mean a lot to you! First, that you made it through and you are still standing. Your story will help someone else get through their troubles.

Therefore, you may be the only person holding you down in the prison of your emotions, I tell you, being alive is a miracle. Think, refocus, look around you and appreciate the beauty of life. God is good and He is loving.

Through having these many encounters, I can attest that the amazing love of God is beyond compare. I dare you to take a plunge!

"Taste and see that the Lord is good; blessed is the man who takes refuge in him." Psalm 34: 8 NIV

It is time to come out of your self-pity party and embrace the true love of God. Love that is unconditional, unfathomable, undeniable, unquenchable and unending. This incomprehensible love of God is the huge connecting valve between Him and mankind.

"But God demonstrates his own love for us in this: While we were still sinners, Christ died for us." Romans 5:8 NIV.

God's love has been made available to all. Any person who becomes well acquainted with this love becomes a translator or the channel through which His kind of love flows. So, the next time you judge someone else's actions, consider their knowledge and appreciation of the love of God. Isn't it pretty amazing that God did not ask us to love Him first but rather to accept this **overwhelming** gesture all for the gain of eternity? This love is **incomparable** to any other type of love; it is **sacrificial**.

"For God so loved the world that he gave his one and only Son, that whoever believes in him shall not perish but have eternal life." John 3:16 NIV

How greatly satisfying that is. Once again someone said

" But I did not ask Jesus to die for me, that is His own problem".

It wasn't His problem; but ours. Still, He took the blame and shame for you and I to be free.

Free from what? Freedom from the guilt of sin, affliction of sickness, pain and diseases.

I know that there are many out there who feel the same way, this is because the natural mind cannot understand the things of the Spirit, and it is only by the spirit can man relate with God.

"But people who aren't spiritual can't receive these truths from God's Spirit. It all sounds foolish to them and they can't understand it, for only those who are spiritual can understand what the Spirit means." 1 Corinthians 2:14 (NLT)

Let your spirit come alive!

"

A man's heart is where life's transactions are initiated, settled and filed, in essence the gate of life

"

Chapter 2: Guard Your Heart!

The heart is a transaction port where life's merchandise is settled. It is the seat of decision making that determines good or bad choices, the battle ground where you can decide to fight or accept defeat.

"Guard your heart!"

This warning came to me while I laid on my hospital bed, recovering from a stroke attack in 2009. I recalled hearing those words before in church but this time it was personal and I knew I needed to heed the warning, so I looked it up from the scriptures.

*Proverbs 4:23 "**Guard your heart** above all else, for it determines the course of your life." (NLT)*

This was one event that changed my life. I became an incurably light-hearted person and learnt to sleep over issues while I let God take charge. I had come to understand and take hold of the key to a healthy relationship with the Father; communicating with Him in prayer.

I had been admitted into hospital for a few weeks, and while I waited for days without any tangible reports from all the several diagnoses done on me, I started getting impatient with my carers. I did not see any reason why I was still being kept in hospital and not discharged. Until one fateful afternoon, while I laid in bed. I felt a tap on my arm, and a gentle whisper speaking to me, asking that I should not be in a hurry to leave for home. The voice then advised, "just pretend as if you are on a vacation; eat, drink, relax and rest." And just as this "visitor" appeared, he was gone. All efforts to identify this stranger failed and no staff on duty matched my description of him. I was then convinced that I had just had a divine visitation from the Lord and realised my being hospitalised was His way of hiding me away and giving me rest I really needed.

There was no doubt in my mind that this was a divine visitation because that was not the first time. I had such an encounter before, I had a similar one a few years before then, also in hospital where I had to refuse a procedure that could have jeopardised the life of my unborn child. With these two episodes and many more I now realise that God chose to speak to me sometimes by sending angels to show up at vital points of decisions for me. I am forever grateful for this.

And so, from then I began to work intentionally to keep my heart free as much as I could with all diligence.

The chain of events that landed me in the hospital started a while back; a time in my life when I was encumbered with so many issues, academic pursuits, while struggling with the demands of motherhood, and laden with the responsibility of being a wife as well as many other unsolicited commitments of life.

I started off towards the kitchen in the early hours of one fateful morning for a cup of coffee but never made it there. The plan was to grab a cup of coffee and head for my study, but just half way down the stairs, I felt my whole body shutting down, not able to speak or call for help, I slumped. By the time I opened my eyes, I was on a stretcher being wheeled across the hospital corridor, there were a couple of medical staff around, I couldn't understand. "What happened?" I asked but only in my thoughts.

I had suffered a stroke, the signs were there, my face dropped, the movements on the left side of my body were slower, my speech was stuttered. While this was going on and I was physically inactive; I heard a loud and clear deep voice in my inner consciousness, my spirit. It sounded like an echo such as you will normally hear in a large empty space; and with exhilarating laughter not audible to anyone else, the voice said:

"This is a lie, there is nothing wrong with you!"

The book of Psalms chapter two flashed through my memory that says;

"Why do the heathen rage and the people imagine a vain thing against the Lord and his anointed.... the Lord shall laugh at their foolishness." Psalm 2:1

Well, that was it, before the doctors arrived for their morning rounds, I was fully recovered, hale and hearty again. And that was the reason I was eager to return home instead of staying in hospital for a couple more weeks; I believed the report of the Lord that divinely assured me of my total healing.

After hearing those words, I did a quick study in relation to the heart. The heart is physically located between the two lungs and protected by the ribs. It pumps blood which carries oxygen to all parts of the body's circulatory system, it propels breathing, eating, drinking, etc.

The heart is also the centre of all thought activities, coordinating the making of decisions, conclusions and executions. So, it is best to be careful about what you allow into your heart because it reflects a whole deal on what comes out or what your life portrays.

The heart must be completely devoted to God and not be torn between the world and Him. Spiritually the heart is the seat of power and a person's greatest asset. The tragedy of our contemporary society today is that it is plagued with people of messed up minds.

"If the word has the potency to revive and make us free, it also has the power to blind, imprison and destroy". **Ralph Ellison**

The hearing ear and the seeing eye are major gateways through which words filter into the heart. Words spoken from time to time have great tendencies of moulding the thoughts in the heart and eventually direct the course of life. A renewed mind sets in motion a transformed life.

Year 2009

Keeping your heart healthy is necessitated by what you feed or allow into your mind. The mind and heart have been used interchangeably in the Word of God and so the same will apply throughout this book. The mind is the processor of your thoughts and emotions. Being at peace with God keeps a settled mind.

Then you will experience God's peace, which exceeds anything we can understand. His peace will guard your hearts and minds as you live in Christ Jesus. Phil 4:7 NLT

This is good news, God speaks to us and attends to our situations consistently, therefore everyone needs their heart regenerated and revived again to heighten the level of perception; because spiritual death and insensitivity was inherited from Adam through sin. To be restored, one only has to believe and have total confidence in the love of God through Jesus Christ.

"Greater love has no man than this, that a man laid down his love for his friends" John 15 :13   NIV

The study of the natural mind identifies different types of **love**, but personally I think that these are only some of the ways in which different emotions are expressed compared to God's compassionate and unconditional love towards us.

Love is more than just a feeling of emotion. Here are a few of what most people understand love to mean.

We are commanded to love God with all our hearts and this is the only means by which human beings could experience God.

First of all, we embrace the love of God in our hearts before it flows into the rest of our bodies and then reflects in our actions and attitudes toward God, His Creations, serving humanity, His works.

According to Proverbs 4:23, we are commanded to watch over our hearts, for from them flow the springs of life. In the NIV, it says, "Above all else, guard your heart, for everything you do flows from it." But when our hearts are not guarded, enemies could erect strongholds in people's hearts using many unnoticeable gimmicks through music we listen to, videos, programmes we watch or the associations we keep, hence the enemy will continue to thrive on unguarded hearts with resultant effects of sin and all its ramifications.

But thanks be to God who has not left us defenceless, He provides divinely powerful weapons for us.

2 Corinthians 10:4 NKJV says:" For the weapons of our warfare are not carnal but mighty in God

for pulling down strongholds". Our weapons and defences are powerful, but we must use them.

Our hearts can be guarded by intentionally controlling our feeds. In other words, what we allow into our hearts through what we listen to and what we look at, will have a great impact in shaping the thoughts of our heart. And this as a result shapes our whole perception of life.

Talking about perception, studies have shown the following different types of love could be expressed and received.

Eros, the Greek god of love and fertility is expressed in romantic sexual passion and desire. ***Philia*** is expressed in friendship and is deemed to be more affectionate in nature. ***Storge*** is a type of familiar love expressed with care and no physical attraction such between Parents and their children and ***Philautia*** on the other hand is a kind of selfish love, it is of the belief that in order to care for others, one must first learn to care for himself.

Agape is love from God to man, the universal, selfless and unconditional love in boundless compassion, it is pure love that accepts, forgives and believes for our greater good. Agape is taught as an innermost personality of God given through His Spirit that spreads to all people.

1John 4:12 -13 NLT *"No one has ever seen God. But if we love each other, God lives in us, and his love is brought to full expression in us. God has given us his Spirit as proof that we live in him and he in us"*

Now with the understanding that God truly loves humanity, should we not also gladly accept and live?

You instinctively become a child of God and a joint heir with Christ when you surrender your life to Him, this means that by divine inheritance you have the same rights as Christ Jesus. How much of this love you have is let out when you have a spirited relationship and a desire to attain a great height with God by having a firm trust in His Word. With that, you become empowered into sonship bearing the mind of Christ, and living with the desire to want to replicate Him to the world. The more you become intimate with God, the more you begin to reflect His personality. "God is love."

Our hearts could be used in the following ways, these are by no means exhaustive

Building Relationships

Relationship is the bridge that connects two or more points of reference, in this instance, God the Creator and mankind His creation. Strength determines the solidity of the bond. Relationships are determined, implying that there are boundaries which define the level of intimacy. But God is limitless and how far we want to go with Him is up to us. God's love is so vast He cannot be contained just like the kids' song says.

Jesus love is very wonderful

It's so high, you can't get over it,

It's so low that you can't get under it

It's so wide you can't get around him,

Oh, wonderful love!

Every relationship needs to be worked on for it to blossom. Building intimacy with God will involve a conscious act of consistent pursuit of His presence in a bid to get to know Him more and more. A lifestyle devoted to steady worship and feasting on the Word daily.

The best way to start to express God is first to imbibe His love and be filled with this nature. And then to increase in knowledge of Him through intimate fellowship with Him so that you must gradually grow to become an expression of Him.

Hence to enjoy the full benefit of Koinonia/ fellowship and partnership in intimacy.

The word **koinonia** is of Greek origin, it simply means Christian fellowship or communion with God

Fellowship and companionship are the major ingredients that feed relationships. God desires that we give Him all our heart, all our soul and all our strength. Total dependence comes from the knowledge that He is all in all, further to this is **Partnership** at His will. We become His hands and feet to reach out to the world at large through a consistent life of **intimacy.**

Deuteronomy 6:5 *"And you must love the Lord your God with all your heart, all your soul, and all your strength."*

„

*Real intimacy can only be
created when relationship
has been established*

„

Chapter 3: Intimacy - The Place To Be

Now that you have knowledge of whom you have encountered and have built the bridge of acquaintances, intimacy is the next step in the process.

To be born and formed according to the purpose of His will requires dying to flesh. Jesus just must be formed in us as was formed in the life of Joseph; every bit of flesh must be crucified.

Relationship patterns however are determined by purpose, love and trust. The more of these ingredients, we accumulate, the stronger the bond of our relationships.

Relationships are a core requirement in human existence; that is why people seek to have perfect and lasting relationships. God created us for fellowship and instituted relationships too. It is therefore important that in our quest for that perfect and long-lasting relationship, careful choices should be made before total commitment is given.

God is able to help one to attain the most desirable level of commitment in any relationship, His love spread throughout humanity when He gave the greatest gift of all. His only begotten Son has saved man from eternal damnation. Then once saved, we ought to reach others with this love.

However, in the world today, there is a plethora of misplaced perception, the love for animals, places, and even inanimate things has heightened against the truth. This is vague, and could be why the writer in the book of Ecclesiastes shares a thought that both humans and animals are subject to the same fate of returning to dust after death though only man will face judgement.

For what happens to the children of man and what happens to the beasts is the same; as one dies, so dies the other. They all have the same breath, and man has no advantage over the beasts, for all is vanity. All go to one place. All are from the dust, and to dust all return. Ecclesiastes 3:19-20

God of Relationship

Right from the beginning, God who was before time, the Father and Originator of all things is the first to express the same.

"This is how much God loved the world: He gave His Son, His one and only Son. And this is why: so that no one need be destroyed; by believing in Him, anyone one can have a whole and lasting life." John 3:16 (paraphrased)

God is a relational God. His kind of relationship is the bedrock of every successful relationship. Not only because it stems from unconditional love, but it is also rich, generous and unending. God's love is the greatest gift ever, and to be connected to His love brings immeasurable blessings.

Oftentimes, I reflect on the ways of love as highlighted through the Word of God to examine my deviations, I can only say to everyone to, look in the mirror and not on others. This way we'll get it right.

"Love never gives up.

Love cares more for others than for self.

Love doesn't want what it doesn't have.

Love doesn't strut,

Doesn't have a swelled head,

Doesn't force itself on others,

Isn't always "me first,"

Doesn't fly off the handle,

Doesn't keep score of the sins of others,

Doesn't revel when others grovel,

Takes pleasure in the flowering of truth,

Puts up with anything,

Trusts God always,

Always looks for the best,

Never looks back,

But keeps going to the end. Love never dies. Inspired speech will be over some day; praying in tongues will end; understanding will reach its limit"

1 Corinthians 13: 4-8 The Message.

This love described in this text only exists in the realm of Christ. No man can be any good by himself for it is beyond his capabilities. Only by the Spirit can we love like this.

Embracing the love of God

Every relationship needs to be fed. While God will always be the first to bring His love to the table; the least you can do is accept it. We may never be able to measure up for what He has done for us but we can at least be grateful for that love.

The book of Genesis recounts that at the cool of the day God would come down to have fellowship with Adam, the first man. It was during one of these sessions that God commissioned Adam in his place of dominion to give names to all His created beings in all spheres - of land, sea and air. This is the gift of relationship, freedom to connect for a good course and not be in isolation.

I often ask myself why it is so difficult for people to accept with open arms the love of God. Truth is that, there is no connectedness where acceptance fails. Every gift is valued when it is received, so is the love of God. While ignorance is a bad feed, sin is an invisible wall that separates and hinders our relationship with God.

Gen3:8a "And they heard the sound of Jehovah God walking up and down in the garden at the breeze of the day: and Adam and his wife hid themselves from the presence of the Lord God"

God offers forgiveness and restoration to get us back to Himself if we are willing to forsake the old ways and embrace His offer of love.

Adam was afraid to relate with God because he felt disconnected the moment sin entered his life. Now we are quick to judge that Adam failed God and humanity. Of course, this is a well-argued theme over time by theologians on clear assertions of deception and disobedience. However, we choose to argue this, it points back to inquire of us about this nature of fallacy since you and I are in the garden of the world today and except salvation comes through Jesus Christ the Saviour, sin would continue to have its course.

This book then has come at such a time, not only as a reminder but also to redirect us to the crux of the matter; going back to the place where we first found love. But for anyone to say they do not need God is foolishness of the heart. God made man to be like Him and gave him the breath of life, the corruption derived from disobedience has set us up for destruction. And unless there is a change of course, the consequence of this separation from God caused by sin; is that man experiences a gradual degeneration from his first breath at birth until he draws his final breath.

Genesis chapter 3 bears record about how the devil beguiled Eve causing her to go against the instructions of God, Eve not only yielded but pulled Adam along. We also ignorantly allow the enemy to do the same to us from time to time by yielding to his enticing falsehood. But God's plan still remains an eternity with Him, found in Christ Jesus through the price of redemption which He paid by laying down His life for the whole world, shedding His blood to redeem whosoever in turn embraces it. This is so amazing! no one should allow themselves to be left out.

Perhaps you are looking for a blissful and fulfilling relationship, either in marriage, family, friendship or any other kind of relationship. Following intimacy with God is the bedrock and greatest motivator of a sound relationship. It will guide you through even the most difficult ones.

" It is for freedom that Christ has set us free. Stand firm, then, and do not let yourselves be burdened again by a yoke of slavery." Galatians 5:1 NIV

This is a stern warning every one of us must heed to. We must be careful not to allow our minds to become enslaved by denominations, doctrines and human philosophies without a solid relationship with God.

Words carefully chosen to condition the mind to react towards the most powerful force on earth is in the will of man. Where there are ethics or principles, they must not be enforced above the Word of God. It is wise not to stand to lose the freedom that Christ has so dearly paid for.

God has ordained kingdom structures that bring liberation from religion, doctrines, sectarianism, we must ensure that we do not get trapped again.

"The most difficult project in the world is the reconstruction of the human mind; it is easier to go to mars than to change the human.". Myles Munroe.

The blessings of relationship with God are beyond measure. He resets your path, aligns and orders your steps to achieving your purpose. But the tragedy of an ignorant mind is great because he fails to see the liberating impact of the truth.

Awake - Understanding Who You Are

Although there are several stages of relationships, the meeting, at which point acceptance is acknowledged, is very important.

There can be no meaningful connection without acceptance. Further to this: interests, enlightenment of purpose and commitment will develop.

This is a wakeup call to everyone; we need to rekindle the ordinance of relationship and fellowship with God our Maker. He is so deeply in love with mankind that is why we must consciously embrace a new walk, new desires and steadfast love for every day to order the course of our lives.

When I consider your heavens, the work of your fingers, the moon and the stars, which you have established [I am constrained to ask]; What is man, that you are mindful of him, and the son of man that you visit [care for] him?" (Psalm 8: 3-4).

This is the right way to ask "why me Lord?". To seek His will through His Word and to lean on him for guidance. We need to be in tune with God for a fulfilling life, seeking his will above all else and asking the kingdom to come on earth, his rulership in all situations ensures a prevailing lifestyle. David's acceptance and acknowledgement as we see in Psalm 8: 3-4 was derived from the awareness of the state he was at.

Remember that the relationship needs to be nourished. The Word of God is the bread of life.

Matthew 4:4 says:

"...It is written, man shall not live by bread alone but by every word that comes from the mouth of God."

The Word of God brings light every day.

Isaiah 50:4b "Morning by morning he awakens; he awakens my ear to hear as those who are taught"

Psalms 119:105 says: "Your word is a lamp to my feet and a light on my path"

No one else is to be blamed when you allow the enemy of our souls; the devil, waste your God given relationships. As in the beginning, the mere fact that the enemy was allowed has caused the damage that only the blood of Jesus could redeem. The conversation that transpired between Eve and the serpent has now translated and multiplied; he still goes about creating havoc everywhere. Do not give the devil a foothold!

There is one truth that is worth embracing, the world will be at peace if we all understand that we are divinely connected with our Maker in all things amidst the warnings of the danger in this world.

Too many of us like Eve are being diverted from their courses in rapidly unimaginable ways than ever because we are not living in the consciousness of the truth, the high moral standards are in a decline mode already.

Oh, how willingly we accept defeat without even trying, when we hold on to the vapour of worldly gains which will pass away and despise eternal life that Christ has richly purchased for us.

God, for love's sake offered Jesus as a token for reconciliation to whosoever believes and accepts such an awesome gift of eternal life. It is through His Spirit, by grace that we first became aware of the need for reconciliation, redemption, restoration and then recovery of our lost position or destiny.

However, eternal life is choice based because man has the free will to choose for himself where he would end up.

I admonish you to choose wisely. At the cross of Jesus were two condemned criminals; one on his left side and the other on the right. Both men exercised their power of choice, while one opted for grace to redemption, the other wallowed in condemnation. But Christ Jesus offers life with no condemnation.

Romans 8:1 "Therefore there is now no condemnation for those who are in Christ Jesus….".

Believe and enter eternity or reject the King of glory and forgo eternity with God. The power of choice can either jeopardise or protect you. I have chosen Life with Christ!

The word of God is a transformer, an agent of change. We begin to lose the nature of sin, the corruption that tends to destroy as we take on

the restored identity of being made in His image and likeness.

So, what to expect when you meet with the Father of all mankind, the King of all the earth is to be changed, and to become anew.

Real relationship

requires

real commitment

Chapter 4: Building Acquaintances

Now that you have let Him into your life, your lifelong affair begins because His intention is to stay with you till eternity, never to be separated again.

Here I am! I stand at the door and knock, if anyone hears my voice and opens the door, I will come in and eat with that person and they with me. Revelation 3:20 NIV

It is then important to get to know Him more and more. With God it promises to be a new experience every day. The more you dig, the more you realise how deep, high, wide His act of love is. It just gets sweeter and sweeter every time.

"Acquaint yourself with God and be at peace, thereby good will come unto you." Job 22:21

I have been born into a church family, schooled in the Bible, baptised and confirmed into the church and have a dedicated life to serve Him. But does this mean that God knows me? Yes, God knows all things, He knew us even before we were born, He formed us and ordered all our parts.

Getting to know Him requires a committed process of seeking and finding Him. Gaining personal knowledge as a result of study, meditation, waiting on Him and above all getting intimate with Him.

Building acquaintances with God shows a desire to see His Kingdom established on earth and His will such as it is in heaven. This is achievable when you play your own part.

Pray

1 Thess. 5:17 admonishes us to *"Pray unceasingly"*. Seeking His will in prayer rather than just asking for a rubber stamp of His approval on your request. If we agree that prayer is a way of communication, then keep asking until your joy is full. The truth is that God speaks to us all the time even when we are not listening.

Study the Word of God

2Tim 2:15 says

"Study to show yourself approved unto God…" you must also know why you are seeking him.

Meditate on His Word.

This involves pondering and soul searching. Joshua 1:8

"This book of the law shall not depart out of your mouth; but thou shalt meditate therein day and night, that thou may observe to do according to all that is written therein; for then thou shalt make thy way prosperous and thou shalt have good success.

Be Obedient to His Word

Doing his bid. Joshua 1:8 emphasises the importance of observing to do according to all that is written in the law of God for prosperity and good success. This includes relationships of any kind as well.

The Joy of Relationship

While at the altar just as in a marriage event, changes come to play. Acceptance is the first step to change: acknowledging the desire for change and being committed to it.

Having a devoted and committed relationship with the Father is more than being a regular church attender because there are many people who go to church meetings, seminars, camps etc. but treat those encounters as casual. This is one area that truly gives me concern and begs the question if these people have truly encountered the Father as they claim. Because if they truly have, there must be a change evident in conjunction with the Word of God.

I would also like to admonish those of us who have truly encountered the Father to be mindful that we do not treat our encounters with the Almighty God with levity.

2 Corinthians 5:17 says:

Therefore, if any man be in Christ, he is a new creature: old things have passed away; behold, all things have become new. Just as there are changes when a new relationship starts with Christ, so are there changes at the onset of many relationships. The first we will consider are the changes at the start of a marriage relationship

- **Name**

The importance of the name we are called cannot be overemphasised. Some destinies have been locked up because of names. A new name comes with a new encounter in Christ. The Bible records several name changes

Abram changed to **Abraham:** There was no way he would have become an exalted father without offspring, so with the change of his name, he was transformed to a father of many nations. See Genesis 17:5

Sarai (quarrelsome) became **Sarah** (noblewoman). Genesis 17:15

Jacob the supplanter was changed to **Israel** the wrestler, he fought for his destiny to be changed. Genesis 32:22-32

Saul was humbled to become Paul when he encountered Jesus on his way to Damascus. The course of his life was altered as he became a preacher of the good news instead of prosecuting the Christians. Acts 9: 1- 9

Congratulations I hereby pronounce you, saved by grace, the Apple of God's eyes, the bride of the lamb", you have a new name **child of God!**

- **Status**

1 Corinthians 6: 17 He who is joined to the Lord becomes one spirit with him.

So, we become saints instead of sinner,

  o   Freed and no longer slaves,

o　Victors and not victims

o　Head and not the tail,

o　More than conquerors in battle

o　Joint heirs with Christ

- **Address**

Secret place of the Most High under the shadow of the Almighty. Psalms 91.

Change of Focus

Trusting Him all the way and not leaning on your own understanding.

Acknowledging Him in all your ways and being directed by Him. Proverbs 3:5.

Looking unto Jesus the Author and finisher of your faith. Hebrews 12:2

- **Responsibilities**

Showing forth His glory, shining His light, pointing direction to His way. Being a good ambassador of His kingdom here on earth. Standing in dominion etc.

- **Priorities**

Following His lead. His ways are not your ways, His thoughts also; so, you become aligned. Your will becomes comfortable to His.

- **Dreams**

You are now in a relationship full of mysteries and so you need to follow His lead perpetually trusting Him all the way. This may be difficult sometimes, but trust is important in relationships and (vows) covenants are meant to be kept even when it hurts. Psalm 15 4b

"…. He who swears to his own hurt and does not change;"

Christ's body - the church is being nurtured to become conformed to the image of Jesus Christ our Lord and Saviour.   This transformation is lifelong if we remain in Him. God is light and therefore walking through him brightens us.

His light comes to shine through us until we become the light.

1 John 3:2

"Beloved, we are now children of God and what we will be has not yet been revealed. We know that when He appears, we will be like Him, for we will see him as he is."

Hallelujah!

Dare to Die Daily

One of the challenges I faced as a young Christian and one that I believe most young Christian's face is stepping forward to the altar whenever a call was made for those who wanted to give their lives to Christ. Certainly, I lost count of how many times I had stepped forward to give my life whenever a call was made. The reason was because I had expected an instant flip of change. It was a while later I realised it was not a hop in and hop out visit to the altar but a stay in process. I had to trust the power of God to effect the change in me.

The altar is a place of humility; where we wait on the Lord and allow the Master to work the wheel of our lives. It is a daily task of refinement, realignment to bring us to perfection until He is ready to present us as a spotless bride.

"

And now abide
faith, hope, love,
these three; but
the greatest of these is
love. 1 Corinthians 13:13 NKJV

"

Chapter 5: Oh, What A Change!

Welcome to a love relationship with the Almighty God who himself is the embodiment of love. God's kind of relationship is centred on love. His love is very powerful, very deep and high and so widely incomparably great! God's love is unexplainable and undeniable! Overwhelming, unending, and non-diminishing.

My earnest prayer for you is one that the Apostle Paul prayed for the church in Ephesus in Ephesians 3:17 - 19.

"So that Christ may dwell in your hearts through faith. And I pray that you, being rooted and established in love, may have power, together with all the Lord's holy people, to grasp how wide and long and high and deep is the love of Christ, and to know this love that surpasses knowledge— that you may be filled to the measure of all the fullness of God." (NIV)

Have you been good to others by showing them kindness? Then you have the power; the power to love, act in love and to receive love that comes from God.

"A *man can receive nothing except it has been given to him from heaven"* John 3:27

This includes the ability to express genuine love of God. A man is unable to love and continue to love genuinely except by divine ability. I have seen people who claim to be once undyingly in love, end up worse haters and hurters. Acquiring the best and most expensive gifts for one does not guarantee or secure love. Things often fall apart, as we face rejection and sometimes are confronted with offences.

Acts 10 :38

How God anointed Jesus Christ with the holy ghost and with power that he went about doing good.

The ability to give and receive love is best expressed through acceptance, nurture and in intimacy. Far away were we when God first extended this love, but the closer we draw to him, the better we are able to grab the love of God and spread it to others.

"But God shows his love for us in that while we were still sinners Christ died for us" Romans 5:8

The Cracked Wall

My marriage relationship was typical of the two sides of a coin. I was so determined to succeed in making it work because I believed in replicating the depth of God's love and the height of forgiveness. Each time I am determined to take every blow, it throws at me with commendable equanimity. After failing several times, and each time beating myself so hard because I could not remain calm and composed. The more I tried to handle confrontations, the more I blew it away uncontrollably. I threw away my peace severally, my cry for help was answered when one day I heard a voice say to me "mend the cracked wall" Whenever a relationship turns sour, it means that there is a cracked wall somewhere. There is no hope in building on the wrong foundation but there is a God who can revisit your past and fix every faulty foundational issue that is wrecking that relationship. If we agree that the whole essence of life is relationship and there is a purpose for our existence, then it is worth asking; what have I been given to benefit from? Everyone is expected to derive some sort of benefit from a relationship; mores especially one formed with the Almighty. When a person entrusts their life to God, there is a natural assurance that from such commitment comes the realisation of their expectations, because there is no hope for a relationship without probity.

As we relate with others, we must acknowledge our differences, and therefore recognise the values in others and appreciate the divine connection that God has ordered; across a type of relationship. Husbands and wives, pastors and their followers, parents and children, employers and their employees, and the list goes on. It is important that we realise that these differences in individuals impose on us a sense of divine responsibility; one that will require individuals to first self-examine themselves before judging others.

The change that you most desire must start from you!

Pain and brokenness is what you feel when things go wrong. Mending the cracks in the walls means revisiting and reversing the cause and effect of something. Trust God to reverse the irreversible.

They that trust in the Lord shall be as mount Zion, which cannot be removed but abideth for ever. As the mountains are round about Jerusalem so the Lord is round about his people from henceforth even forever. Ps 125:1-2 NIV

The Quest

It is often said that there is no vacuum in nature. Everyone seeks fulfilment in something known or unknown.

For me, the quest from all surrounding facts of life is that while I am still breathing, believing, following, is to continually long for Him; my God until the day I see Him face to face.

For no one knows what He is like, though we understand that we are made in His image and fashioned in His likeness but this we know that when He shall appear we shall be like Him. How I long for that day.

Are you expecting the Lord soon? Because He is definitely coming for those who are earnestly expecting His return and as well, for those who are adamant of this truth.

If you are, then how prepared are you now?

No one can see Him without holiness. He is purer than light to behold iniquity, the slightest sinner man cannot stand in His presence. The question is how can I live in this world so full of filth, confusion, sin, corruption and yet stay pure? it is by believing in our hearts and living what we believe and not simply what we say.

"How can a young person stay on the path of purity? By living according to your word. I seek you with all my heart; do not let me stray from your commands." Psalm 119: 9-10

"Blessed are those who hunger and thirst for righteousness, for they will be filled." Matthew 5:6

Everyone that comes to the Lord expects to fill a hollow and be made whole, to be restored to the original state - the image of God. This may be physical or spiritual, it stems from the desire for peace, healing, strength to overcome a challenge, assistance or help in time of need. No man is created to be empty. God would come to have fellowship with Adam in the garden according to the book of Genesis to satisfy his soul but as Adam lost this place to sin, loneliness crept in due to the loss of fellowship with God.

That vacuum that God created in man must always be filled or else one entirely feels empty and void. Everyone wants to be the highest truest expression of themselves but due to gross deception many have resorted, to drugs, alcohol, slavery to undeserved gods by engaging in wicked activities, justifying immorality that only have momentary gratification but eternal consequences. Beware!
You cannot put a square peg in a round hole, that hollow can only be filled by the One who created it in the first place.
Ecclesiastes 3:11 says: *"He has made everything beautiful in its time. **He has also set eternity in the***

human heart*; yet no one can fathom what God has done from beginning to end."*

There is a way that appears to be right, but in the end, it leads to death. Proverbs 14:12

But Jesus said...

"I am the way and the truth and the life. No one comes to the Father except through me." John 14:6

Abraham, a perfect example, was a descendant of Ur of the Chaldeans, his fathers were idol worshippers, but deep inside of him was a quest to know the true God. He knew there was something beyond what he could see, deep inside he yearned for the unknown God. He felt empty until he had an encounter.

I deeply pray and heartily believe for the one reading this book to encounter this loving God. It will build your trust, stir your hope and boost your confidence when you know in whom you believe.

The more you seek Him, to know the length, the width, the height and depth of Him and to be filled with the measure of all His fullness, the more He pours of Himself into you and satisfies the longing of your heart.

Psalm 107:9

"For He satisfies the longing soul, and fills the hungry soul with goodness."

God's desire is not only to fill you up but for you to be filled beyond capacity...
Overflow

Chapter 6: Entering into Your Overflow

God's desire is not only to fill you up but for you to be filled beyond capacity. To overflow simply means to be a super- abundant continuo. Life is more meaningful when you reach out to others in whichever capacity you find yourself. Just that simple smile is given to you to inspire someone else.

What then is required of us to reach the point of this overflow?

Your thirst depends on how empty your jar is, for instance if your jar is three quarters full, you will only need one quarter to fill up and your thirst may not be as strong as if you had been nine tenth empty. Therefore, to ensure that your jar needs continual fill, you must have other jars attached. This is because a jar with many holes will be a channel to spread many arounds for others to be filled. Being a jar with many holes may be a painful process but remember that it is a sacrifice with its blessings.

"Whoever believes in me, as the Scripture has said, rivers of living water will flow from within them." John 7:38

You must be a willing channel to others while you let Him do the filling.

Your thirst is quenched not by the eagerness to tap into every resource available to you like the sermons, teachings, tapes you have listened to but that God-sized vacuum within every soul can only be filled by the true revelation that comes to an individual by the Spirit of God within him.

Having a deep inward affection towards God based on personal revelation, testimonies and experience with all conscious passion, is the conduit by which the Almighty fills us up.

The resources we have available to us today are good and have their purposes. Jesus when He was on earth from time to time sat to teach and performed all the miracles while his followers watched closely. However, everything they learnt remained head knowledge, and the sheer joy of being known among the crowd as close allies with Jesus and nothing more.

Like them, sometimes we have been with Him for so long and yet do not understand Him in our hearts, you could imagine what went on in their heart when He taught them about destroying the temple and rebuilding it in three days, or when He reiterated that the hour had come. They hardly understood Him until He was sentenced to a gruesome death on the cross and witnessed the excruciating pain of torture.

This was evident in the many questions they asked in confusion.

Thomas said to him, *"Lord, we don't know where you are going, so how can we know the way?" John 14:5*

Philip said, *"Lord, show us the Father and that will be enough for us." John 14:8*

Jesus saw how Philip had been with him for so long and yet had not known Him.

The events that came afterwards triggered something in them that they began to yearn for such an experience as to be with Him again and now with a better understanding of purpose. Then their thirst kept them tarrying in fellowship until such a time that the promised Holy Spirit came and every one had an encounter as recorded in Acts 2.

When you come to terms with the reality of the indwelling of the Spirit within you, there is an outpouring of the Holy Spirit. His seed grows and springs from within you to overflow. This supernatural infilling comes with the divine enabling grace that is needed to function in all aspects of life. It is the anointing of the Holy Spirit!

"How God anointed Jesus of Nazareth with the Holy Spirit and power, and how he went around doing good and healing all who were under the power of the devil, because God was with him" *Acts 10:38a.*

This is overflowing!
God be with you

Maranatha!

Lessons In Life

*L*ife is not a rehearsal but an interesting journey. Everyone you meet has a part to play, be it positive or negative because everyone has a different perspective to life.

You cannot stop how people behave to you but you can decide how you react to it. Wisdom is profitable to direct.

Things are not always the way they seem to be. There are three sides to a coin, the upside, downside and the inside. The real value is always the hidden part.

Do everything without vainglory, the ultimate goal is not to please man but God.

Judging too soon has a way of putting you in the guilty box.

www.ingramcontent.com/pod-product-compliance
Lightning Source LLC
Chambersburg PA
CBHW061326120726
48001CB00002B/716